STARK LIBRARY   JUL   2021

Y0-CJG-720

IN FOCUS...
DAWN OF THE DINOSAURS

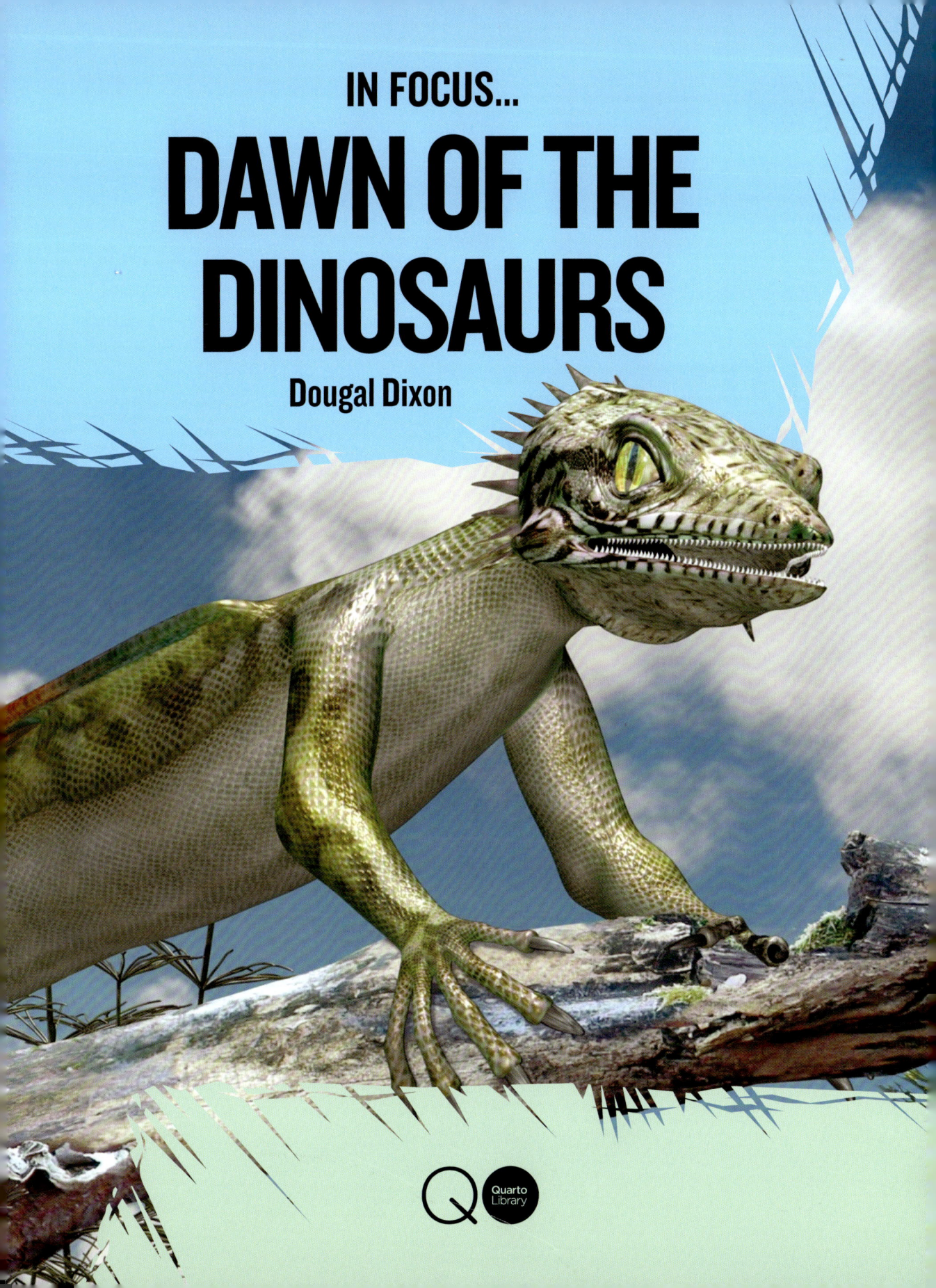

Dougal Dixon

Quarto Library

Quarto is the authority on a wide range of topics.
Quarto educates, entertains and enriches the lives of our readers—enthusiasts and lovers of hands-on living.
www.quartoknows.com

This library edition published in 2020
by Quarto Library,
an imprint of The Quarto Group.
26391 Crown Valley Parkway,
Suite 220
Mission Viejo, CA 92691, USA
T: +1 949 380 7510
F: +1 949 380 7575
www.QuartoKnows.com

© 2020 Quarto Publishing plc

All rights reserved. No part of this publication may be reproduced, stored in a retrieval system, or transmitted in any form or by any means, electronic, mechanical, photocopying, recording, or otherwise, without the prior permission of the publisher, nor be otherwise circulated in any form of binding or cover other than that in which it is published and without a similar condition being imposed on the subsequent purchaser.

Distributed in the United States and Canada by
Lerner Publisher Services
241 First Avenue North
Minneapolis, MN 55401 U.S.A.
www.lernerbooks.com

A CIP record for this book is available from the Library of Congress.

ISBN: 978 0 7112 4808 3

Manufactured in Guangdong, China CC042020

9 8 7 6 5 4 3 2 1

CONTENTS

*Words in **bold** are explained in the Glossary on page 31.*

LIFE BEGINS 4

THE FIRST REPTILES 6

SWAMP LIFE 8

300 MILLION YEARS AGO 10

SYNAPSIDS 12

REAL REPTILES 14

DIMETRODON 16

TEETH AND TUSKS 18

DAWN OF THE DINOSAURS 20

CREATURES OF THE COAST 22

TRIASSIC SEA MONSTERS 24

FISH LIZARDS 26

RISE OF THE DINOSAURS 28

GLOSSARY 31

INDEX 32

LIFE BEGINS

DINO DATA
The earliest form of life on Earth was **bacteria**. Bacteria **fossils** have been found that are 3.7 billion years old!

Dinosaurs first appeared on land at least 230 million years ago, but life probably began in the oceans. The first living things appeared at least 3.5 billion years before dinosaurs.

Soft-bodied animals

The first sea creatures to emerge had no backbone or shell. They had soft bodies, like a jellyfish. These early life forms came in different shapes and sizes. Some were just blobs. Others were shaped like wavy stripes or ribbons.

The first sea creatures with shells developed about 540 million years ago. Some of these were mollusks, like today's snails.

On dry land

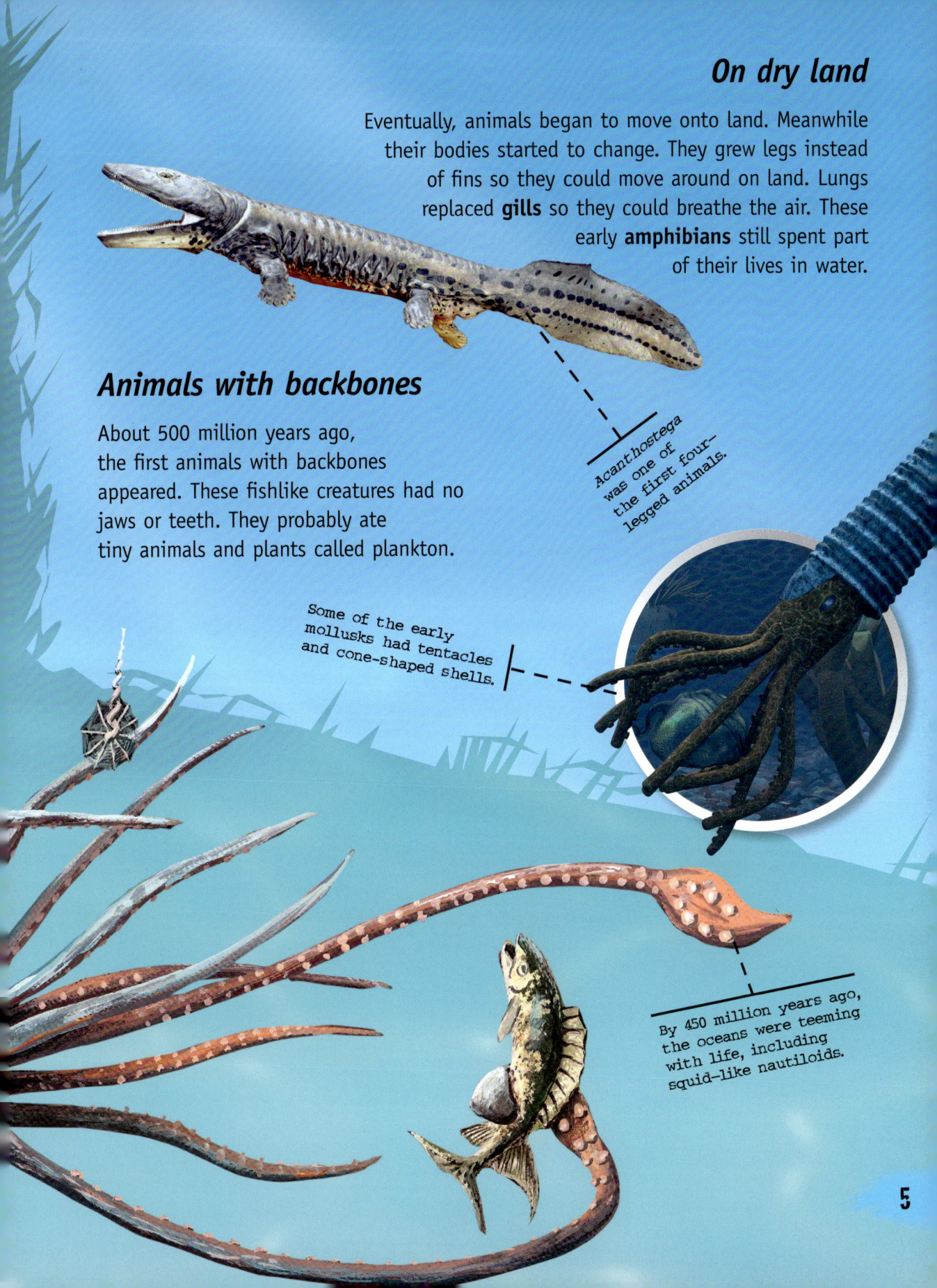

Eventually, animals began to move onto land. Meanwhile their bodies started to change. They grew legs instead of fins so they could move around on land. Lungs replaced **gills** so they could breathe the air. These early **amphibians** still spent part of their lives in water.

Acanthostega was one of the first four-legged animals.

Animals with backbones

About 500 million years ago, the first animals with backbones appeared. These fishlike creatures had no jaws or teeth. They probably ate tiny animals and plants called plankton.

Some of the early mollusks had tentacles and cone-shaped shells.

By 450 million years ago, the oceans were teeming with life, including squid-like nautiloids.

5

THE FIRST REPTILES

Millions of years passed. Some amphibians began to develop features that made them more suited to life on land. By 300 million years ago, these had become the first true **reptiles**. It was from these early animals that the great dinosaurs eventually **evolved**.

Adapting to land

Early reptiles had sturdy legs that were perfect for moving on solid ground. They snapped up insects with their strong teeth or fed on the lush plants that covered the planet. Unlike amphibians, which laid their soft eggs in water, early reptiles laid hard-shelled eggs that could survive on land.

Reptile eggs had a tough shell. This protected the baby inside and stopped the egg from drying out.

Scutosaurus was a large early reptile that grew up to 8 feet (2.4 meters) long.

DINO DATA

A lot of early reptiles had several rows of very sharp teeth. This helped them crush up animals such as snails and grind up plants to eat.

Giant reptiles

Many early reptiles looked like modern lizards, but others were bigger, with bony armor, spikes, and horns. *Scutosaurus* had a massive body and a heavy, spiked head. It probably moved very slowly because it weighed so much.

Scientists are not sure whether *Westlothiana* was an amphibian or an early reptile.

SWAMP LIFE

When the first reptiles appeared, there was more oxygen on Earth than there is today. This helped plants and animals grow to enormous sizes. Giant plants such as horsetails, ferns, and moss covered the land in a thick, green carpet.

Huge creatures similar to spiders lived in the murky forest undergrowth.

Fossil finds

Some amazing fossils have been found at a place called Joggins in Canada. This was once a **prehistoric** swamp. Here, inside ancient tree stumps, scientists discovered the remains of nearly 200 amphibians. These animals may have died when a forest fire swept through the swamp.

Hylonomus

Scientists at Joggins also found fossils of *Hylonomus*. This is the first known creature with a backbone that could live entirely on land. *Hylonomus* was a lizard-like animal with thick, scaly skin. Its teeth were simple spikes, but some of the front ones were longer than the rest. *Hylonomus* used these for gripping its insect **prey**.

Early reptiles such as *Hylonomus* had boxlike skulls.

Incredible insects

Millions of insects and spiders lived in ancient swamps and forests. They were huge compared to modern insects. Some of the most amazing creatures were giant dragonflies that were the size of birds.

The plants in warm, damp swamps provided food and shelter for insects, attracting reptiles.

DINO DATA

Venomous prehistoric centipedes and deadly scorpions could grow up to 3 feet (1 meter) long!

300 MILLION YEARS AGO

The history of Earth is divided into chunks of time called periods. Most early reptiles developed during the Permian period, from 300 million to 250 million years ago.

Hot and cold

During the Permian period, different places on Earth had very different **climates**. The south was cold and dry and the north had extreme seasons that were very wet or very dry. On land there were large areas of hot, dry desert.

DINO DATA
Of all the species that lived in the Permian period, only 4 percent survived into the following Triassic period.

Plant-eating reptiles were common, and so were the meat-eaters that hunted them!

Reptile survival

Reptiles adapted to survive in places where amphibians could not. Amphibians needed to spend time in the water. The skin of reptiles could hold in moisture, so these animals were able to live in hot places.

The therapsid *Procynosuchus* had webbed feet, which helped it swim.

The "Great Dying"

At the end of the Permian period, nearly all life on Earth was wiped out. This is called the "Great Dying." Perhaps volcanoes pumped ash into the air, blocking out the Sun. Maybe animals could not adapt quickly enough to the changing climate. No one really knows what happened.

Some scientists think a huge volcano erupted at the end of the Permian period.

SYNAPSIDS

Early reptiles began to develop in different ways. A group called synapsids had a different-shaped skull from other reptiles. Their jaws were much more powerful and could open wide to catch larger prey. Synapsids were the **ancestors** of today's mammals.

DINO DATA

Anapsids were the very first reptiles. They had heavy, square skulls. Later reptiles, such as the pelycosaurs, had much lighter skulls.

Many pelycosaur fossils have been found in ancient swamps in North America.

Basin lizards

Synapsids are split into two groups: the early pelycosaurs and the later therapsids. The word pelycosaur means "basin lizard." They developed about 300 million years ago. Pelycosaurs started out as small creatures. Later, they developed into much bigger, heavier, and stronger animals.

Ophiacodon's back legs were longer than its front legs, so it was probably a good runner.

Feeding habits

Pelycosaurs were good survivors. This was because each type had special teeth that suited its diet. Most had strong jaws, but they did not all feast on other land animals. Some, such as *Ophiacodon*, caught fish in swamps or rivers. Others only ate plants.

As well as helping it warm up or cool down, Edaphosaurus's sail might have been used to attract mates or scare off enemies.

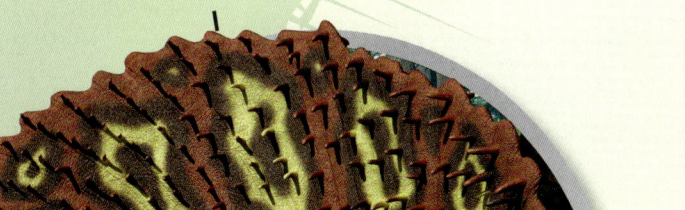

Size and shape

Different pelycosaurs had different physical features. Some of them were only a few inches long, but others grew to more than 10 feet (3 meters). They looked very similar to modern lizards, but some pelycosaurs, such as *Dimetrodon* and *Edaphosaurus*, also had large "**sails**" on their backs.

13

REAL REPTILES

Most modern reptiles belong to a group called diapsids. These animals are very important in the history of Earth, because they are also the ancestors of the dinosaurs.

DINO DATA

Diapsids had special muscles in their jaws that allowed them to open their mouths extra wide and snap them shut hard.

Petrolacosaurus lived at the end of the Carboniferous period, about 302 million years ago.

Habitats

Diapsids developed features that helped them survive in different **habitats**. *Araeoscelis* had long legs, so it could run fast. This helped it catch insects such as beetles in dry desert areas. *Coelurosauravus* glided from tree to tree in its forest home. *Askeptosaurus* lived in water. It had a ribbon-like tail that helped it swim.

Askeptosaurus's webbed feet were perfect for steering through water.

Coelurosauravus's "wings" were flaps of skin attached to long, rib-like bones, which stretched out on the sides of its body.

Petrolacosaurus

Petrolacosaurus is the first-known diapsid. It looked a lot like a modern lizard, except that its legs were longer. Its tail was as long as its body and head put together. *Petrolacosaurus* was an insect-hunter.

15

DIMETRODON

Dimetrodon was one of the most powerful pelycosaurs. This large, meat-eating animal lived about 280 million years ago. It has been nicknamed "finback" because of its large sail.

Dimetrodon lived in North America 50 million years before the dinosaurs.

DINO DATA

Dimetrodon's sharp front teeth were good for tearing meat off its prey. It also had special teeth for grinding flesh and bone.

Warming up and cooling down

In the morning, *Dimetrodon* stood with its sail facing the rising Sun. The Sun would warm the sail, which warmed up *Dimetrodon's* whole body. To cool down, *Dimetrodon* moved its sail to catch a cooling wind.

Top predator

Dimetrodon's name means "two types of teeth." This animal was a carnivore (meat-eater). It probably ate whatever it could catch. This could be insects, amphibians, and even other pelycosaurs.

Getting around

Dimetrodon's legs were not directly beneath its body. They were set on the sides. This meant that *Dimetrodon* walked close to the ground, more like a crocodile than a dinosaur.

Dimetrodon could grow to 10 feet (3 meters) long, and the sail on its back could be more than 3 feet (1 meter) tall.

Dimetrodon's sail was made of long spines that came out of its backbone.

TEETH AND TUSKS

During the Permian period, one group of pelycosaurs began to evolve and became the ancestors of mammals. These animals are called therapsids. They probably had hair and were equipped with teeth and tusks.

DINO DATA

Lycaenops ("wolf face") worked together in packs to attack and kill prehistoric animals much larger than themselves.

Moschops may have fought by head-butting each other with their huge, thick skulls.

Types of teeth

Like pelycosaurs, most therapsids had powerful jaws and very sharp teeth. They used their front teeth for attacking and tearing at their prey. Their cheek teeth were used for chopping and grinding food.

Therapsids with tusks

The therapsids *Dicynodon* and *Kannemeyeria* belonged to a group that had two strong tusks. Scientists call these animals dicynodonts, which means "two dog teeth." These tusks were probably used to dig up plants and roots.

Plant-eating *Dicynodon* had two tusks and a horny beak, but it had almost no other teeth.

Holes in the head

All therapsids had a pair of holes on each side of their skull, behind the eyes. These holes made the skull lighter and the jaws stronger. Once the dinosaurs evolved millions of years after the therapsids, they had a different arrangement of holes in their skulls.

DAWN OF THE DINOSAURS

The Triassic period began about 250 million years ago, when the Earth had one giant **continent**. This meant that animals and plants could spread easily across the world.

A warm world

There were no frozen ice caps at the North Pole and South Pole, like there are today. A lot of land was desert. There was still some rain, though. Plants grew around the lakes and pools formed by the rain. This plant life attracted ancient animals.

Coelophysis probably lived in forests, hunting in packs.

Gracilisuchus was a small, crocodile-like animal that could run on its back legs.

Earth changes

By the end of the Triassic period, the land was starting to break up. Two smaller continents eventually formed, with an ocean between them. The weather changed, too. As it became cooler and wetter, more and more reptiles evolved.

Triassic life

Reptiles ruled Earth during the Triassic period. Ichthyosaurs and nothosaurs swam in Triassic seas. Crocodiles and lizards hunted on land. Toward the end of this period, the dinosaurs, the greatest of all reptiles, finally appeared.

Tanystropheus's neck was much longer than its body and tail put together.

DINO DATA

The earliest dinosaurs were found in South America.

21

CREATURES OF THE COAST

Over millions of years, many animals adapted to life on land. But during the Triassic period, a group of reptiles called placodonts went back to the seas. Their bodies changed again to suit life in the water.

Henodus had the same body shape as a modern turtle. It was as wide as it was long.

Hunting shellfish

Placodonts lived in shallow waters or on the shore. They did not go out into very deep water. Instead, they swam along the coast. They used their broad teeth to grind up the shellfish that they found there. Many placodonts had hard shells, like modern turtles. These protected their soft bodies from attack by predators.

Placodus used its front row of blunt teeth to pull shellfish off rocks.

Placochelys

Placochelys was well-adapted to life in the seas. It had a body like a turtle and was covered in tough, knobby plates. These made a protective body armor.

Placochelys had a short tail and paddle-like legs for swimming.

DINO DATA

Despite their similar appearance, placodonts are not related to turtles. They happened to develop the same body shape and live in similar environments.

Henodus

Henodus was a large placodont. It had a huge, square body and a small, square head, like today's turtles. Its back and belly were covered in bony plates. These protected it from attack by other sea animals, such as the ichthyosaurs.

TRIASSIC SEA MONSTERS

The fish-eating nothosaurs lived and died out during the Triassic period. Scientists think they might have been a "halfway stage" between the land reptiles and the sea reptiles called plesiosaurs.

Nothosaurus's feet had five long, webbed toes.

Pistosaurus had a mouth full of sharp, pointed teeth for eating fish.

Great lengths

Nothosaurs had long, bendy bodies and tails. They stretched out their long necks to snap up passing fish. Their strong jaws and sharp teeth killed their prey instantly.

Useful flippers

Nothosaurs' front flippers were stronger than their back ones. They used their front flippers for steering, braking, and turning quickly in the water. Some nothosaurs had webbed feet with toes like a duck, but others had smoother flippers like a seal.

Pistosaurus

Pistosaurus was an unusual sea reptile. Its body was like a nothosaur's, but it flew through the water with wing-like flippers. This was how the plesiosaurs swam. Nothosaurs swam by moving their bodies from side to side. *Pistosaurus* would have snatched up fish in its powerful jaws.

Not all nothosaurs were giants. Little *Lariosaurus* grew to only 2 feet (0.6 meter) long.

DINO DATA

Nothosaurs lived in the water, but they came on shore to lay their eggs and to sunbathe!

FISH LIZARDS

DINO DATA
Most ichthyosaurs were **extinct** by the end of the Jurassic period. Only a few survived into the Cretaceous period.

The name ichthyosaur means "fish lizard." This suits the ichthyosaurs. They lived in the water and had some fishlike features, such as their body shape, but they were actually reptiles.

With their slim bodies, many ichthyosaurs looked similar to dolphins.

Speedy swimmers

Ichthyosaurs could swim very fast. They darted through the water at over 25 miles (40 kilometers) per hour. They used their fishlike tail to move so quickly, thrashing it from side to side like a shark does today.

Big and small

The enormous *Shonisaurus* was the largest of the ichthyosaurs. This Triassic marine reptile could grow up to 50 feet (15 meters) long. There were several enormous types of ichthyosaur in the Triassic oceans. Compared to the huge *Shonisaurus*, *Mixosaurus* was a tiny creature that only grew to about 3 feet (1 meter) long. Fossils of this little ichthyosaur have been found all over the world, from China to Alaska.

The giant *Shonisaurus* only had teeth at the front of its mouth.

Deep divers

Ichthyosaurs ate fish and squid. The teeth of some early species suggest that they may also have crushed and eaten shellfish. They could dive deeper than other marine reptiles, so they could catch prey that other ocean hunters could not reach.

RISE OF THE DINOSAURS

The first true dinosaurs had appeared during the Triassic, including the sauropodomorph dinosaurs. When the world's climate began to change dramatically, the dinosaurs were quick to adapt. Soon they were poised and ready to rule the world.

Mussaurus ("mouse lizard") lived in South America during the Jurassic period.

Early Sauropodomorph features

Sauropodomoprhs were plant-eating dinosaurs. The most primitive of them ranged from cat-sized creatures to some that were over 30 feet (9 meters) long. They moved about on either their hind legs or on all fours.

Anchisaurus may have moved about on two legs as well as four.

DINO DATA

Climate change at the end of the Triassic caused the extinction of 75 percent of all species.

Plateosaurus's tail made up half its length.

Plateosaurus

Plateosaurus was a large example of an early sauropodomorph that lived on the **plains** of Europe in late Triassic times. It probably traveled in herds, looking for new feeding grounds. It moved on all four legs most of the time, but could also stand up on its back legs. This helped *Plateosaurus* feed from higher branches.

PICTURE CREDITS

Key: FC = front cover, BC = back cover, t = top, b = bottom, c = center, r = right, l = left.

Alamy:
5cr Stocktrek Images, Inc; 7tr Stocktrek Images, Inc; 8-9 Stocktrek Images, Inc; 13 bl Stocktrek Images, Inc; 21c Friedrich Sawyer; 26bl Stocktrek Images, Inc.

Beehive Illustration:
9tr Lazlo Veres; 20-21 Mark Turner.

Dreamstime:
26-27 Mr1805, 27tr Mr1805; 28-29 Mr1805, 29c Mr1805.

Getty Images:
2 Dorling Kindersley; 6c Louie Psihoyos; 10-11 Corbis/Walter Myers/Stocktrek Images; 16-17 Corbis/Jerry LoFaro/Stocktrek Images, 17tl Dorling Kindersley; 19cl Corbis/Kostyantyn Ivanyshen; 22-23 DEA Picture Library; 28bl Corbis/Louie Psihoyos.

Natural History Museum:
5t The Trustees of the Natural History Museum.

Science Photo Library:
1 Natural History Museum, London; 4-5 Richard Bizley; 8tr Richard Bizley; 12 Christian Jegou Publiphoto Diffusion; 14-15 Natural History Museum, London; 18-19 Christian Jegou Publiphoto Diffusion; 22br Jaime Chirinos; 24-25 Jaime Chirinos; 30-31 Christian Jegou Publiphoto Diffusion.

Shutterstock:
FC b/g Herschel Hoffmeyer, FC (main) Catmando; BC Daniel Eskridge; 11cl Pichugin Dmitry.

Wikipedia:
17cr

The publisher gratefully acknowledges the permission granted to reproduce the copyright material in this book. Every effort has been made to trace copyright holders and to obtain their permission for the use of copyright material. The publisher apologizes for any errors or omissions in the above list and would be grateful if notified of any corrections that should be incorporated in future reprints or editions of this book.

GLOSSARY

amphibian
an animal that has a moist skin and lays its eggs in water; amphibians spend the first part of their lives in water but usually live on land as adults

ancestor
an early type of animal that evolved into other, similar types of animal

bacteria
tiny, simple organisms (living things) that live almost everywhere on Earth

climate
the pattern of weather that is common in one place over a long period of time

continent
a very large area of land surrounded by ocean

evolves
changes over time to adapt to new conditions and survive

extinct
there are no members of this type, or species, of animal still alive

fossil
the remains of a long-dead animal or plant that have, over time, been turned into stone

gills
breathing organs found in many animals that live in water

habitat
the place where an animal or plant lives

plain
a large, flat area of land with few trees

prehistoric
describes a time long before humans lived on Earth, or could write about the world

prey
an animal that is hunted by other animals for food

reptile
a scaly-skinned animal; most reptiles lay their eggs on land although some reptiles give birth instead

sail
a large, fin-like structure on the back of some prehistoric reptiles

31

INDEX

Acanthostega 5
amphibians 5, 6, 7, 8, 11, 17
anapsids 12
Anchisaurus 29
Araeoscelis 15
armor 7, 23
Askeptosaurus 15

backbones 5, 9, 17
bacteria 4

Carboniferous period 14
centipedes 9
climate change 11, 21, 28, 29
Coelophysis 20
Coelurosauravus 15
continents 20, 21
Cretaceous period 26
crocodiles 21

diapsids 14–15
Dicynodon 19
dicynodonts 19
Dimetrodon 13, 16–17
dinosaurs, evolution of 6, 14, 19, 21, 28–29
dragonflies 9

early life forms 4–5
Edaphosaurus 13
eggs 6, 25
extinctions, mass 11, 29

first living things 4
fossils 4, 8, 9, 12, 27

Gracilisuchus 21
"Great Dying" 11

Henodus 22, 23
herds 29
horns 7
Hylonomus 9

ichthyosaurs 21, 23, 26–27
insects 9, 15, 17

Jurassic period 26

Kannemeyeria 19

Lariosaurus 25
Lycaenops 18

mammals 12, 18
marine animals 22–27
Mixosaurus 27
mollusks 4, 5
Moschops 18
Mussaurus 28

nautiloids 5
nothosaurs 21, 24–25
Nothosaurus 24

Ophiacodon 13
oxygen 8

pack hunters 18, 20

pelycosaurs 12, 13, 16–19
Permian period 10–11, 18
Petrolacosaurus 14
Pistosaurus 24, 25
Placochelys 23
placodonts 22–23
Placodus 22
plankton 5
plants 8, 9
Plateosaurus 29
plesiosaurs 24, 25
Procynosuchus 11

reptiles 6–7, 8, 9, 10, 11, 12, 14–15, 21, 22, 24, 25, 26, 27

sails 13, 16, 17
sauropodomorphs 28–29
scorpions 9
Scutosaurus 7
Shonisaurus 27
spiders 8, 9
spikes 7
swamps 8–9, 12, 13
synapsids 12–13

Tanystropheus 21
teeth 6, 7, 9, 13, 16, 18, 19, 22, 24, 25, 27
therapsids 11, 13, 18–19
Triassic period 10, 20–21, 22, 24, 28, 29
turtles 22, 23
tusks 19

volcanoes 11

Westlothiana 7

3 1333 05078 8734